Blue Sky

THE PEANUTS MOVIE
by SCHULZ

MUSIC FROM THE MOTION PICTURE SOUNDTRACK

ISBN 978-1-4950-5242-2

HAL•LEONARD® CORPORATION
7777 W. BLUEMOUND RD. P.O. BOX 13819 MILWAUKEE, WI 53213

Visit Hal Leonard Online at
www.halleonard.com

CONTENTS

LINUS AND LUCY

By VINCE GUARALDI

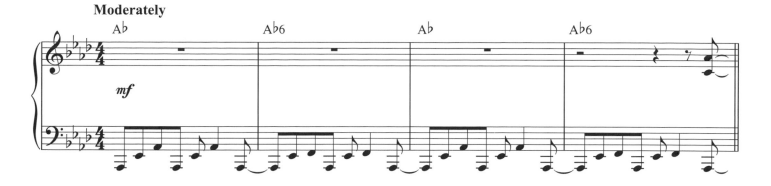

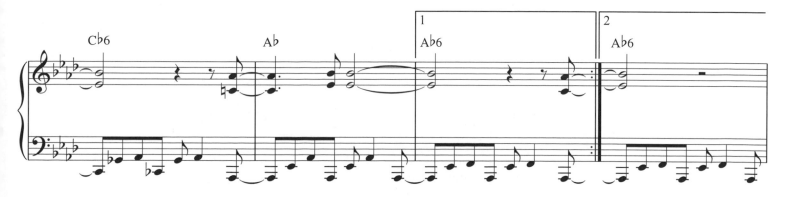

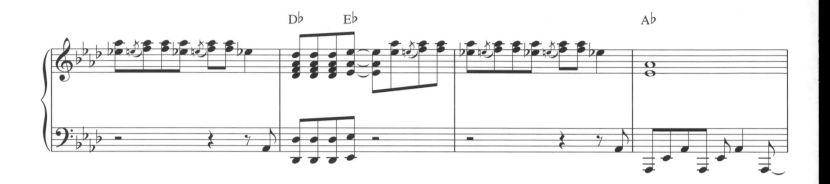

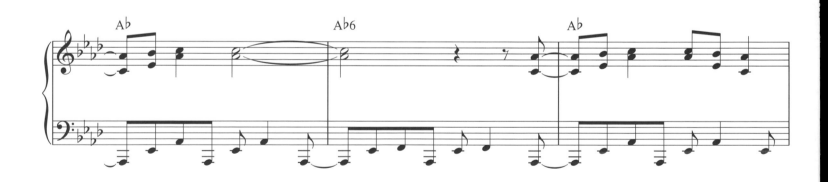

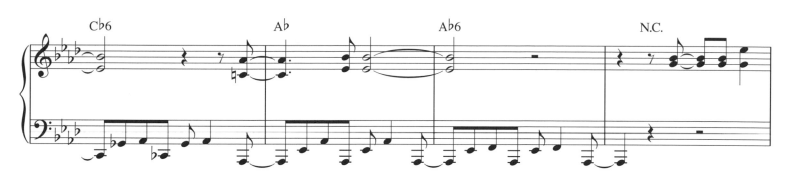

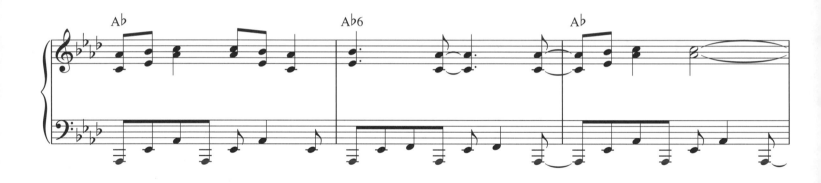

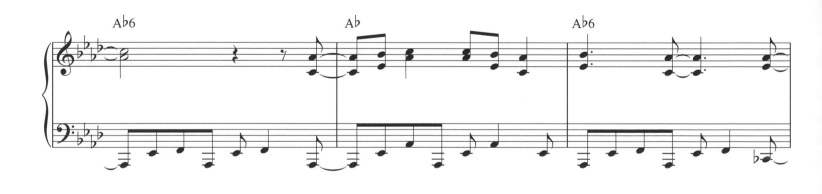

Swing feel (♩♩ = ♩³♪)

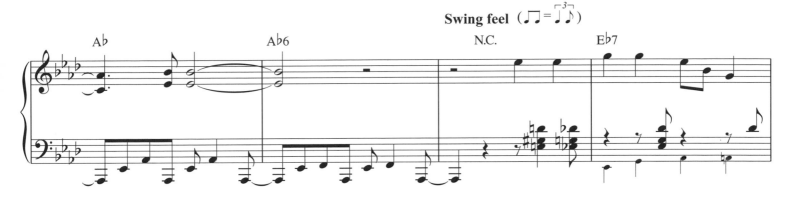

14

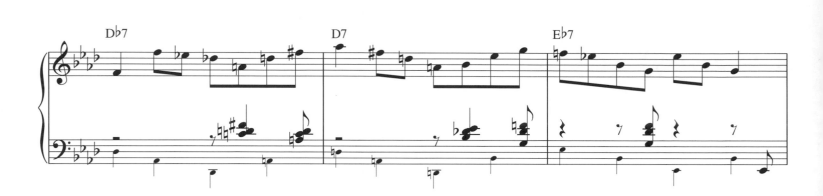

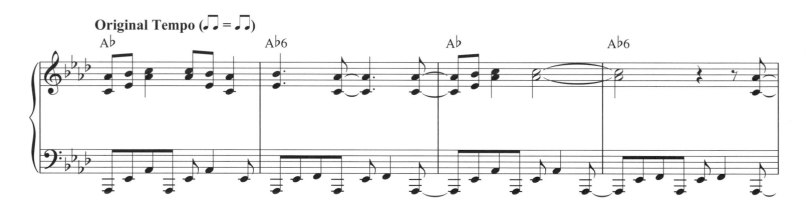

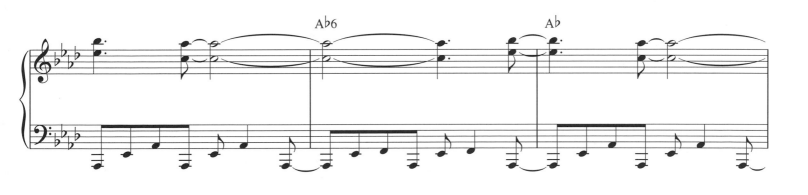

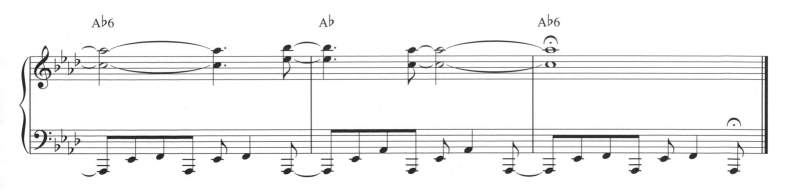

BETTER WHEN I'M DANCIN'

Words and Music by MEGHAN TRAINOR
and THADDEUS DIXON

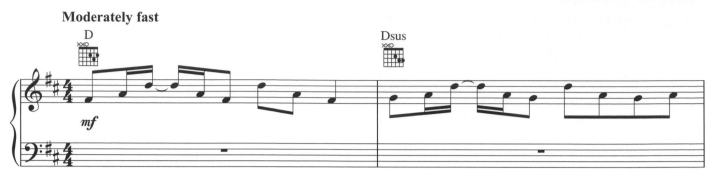

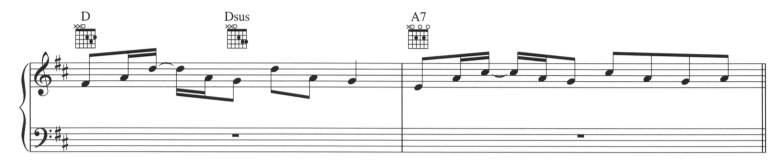

Don't think a - bout it, just move your bod - y.
When you fi - n'lly let go, and you slay that so - lo,

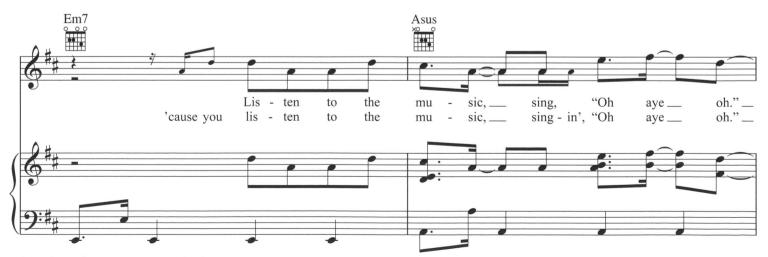

Lis - ten to the mu - sic, ___ sing, "Oh aye ___ oh." ___
'cause you lis - ten to the mu - sic, ___ sing - in', "Oh aye ___ oh." ___

*Lead vocal written an octave higher.

you, but I feel bet - ter when I'm danc - in', yeah, yeah. ___ I'm bet - ter when I'm

dance - in', yeah, yeah. ___

And we ___ can do this to - geth - er.
(D.S.) we ___ can do this to - geth - er.

I bet ___ you feel bet - ter when you're danc - in', yeah, yeah. ___
Bet ___ you feel bet - ter when you're danc - in', yeah, yeah. ___

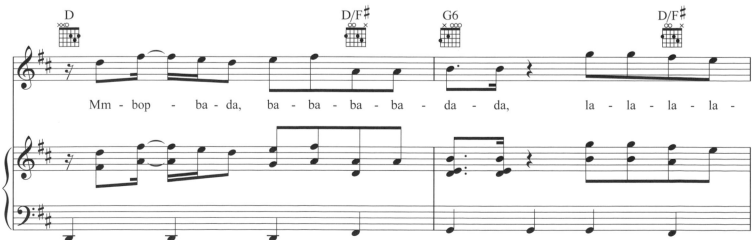

Mm - bop - ba - da, ba - ba - ba - ba - da - da, la - la - la - la -

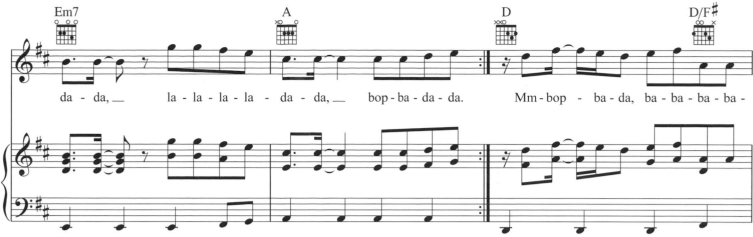

da - da, __ la - la - la - la - da - da, __ bop - ba - da - da. Mm - bop - ba - da, ba - ba - ba - ba -

da - da, la - la - la - la - da - da, __ la - la - la - la - da - da, __ bop - ba - da - da.

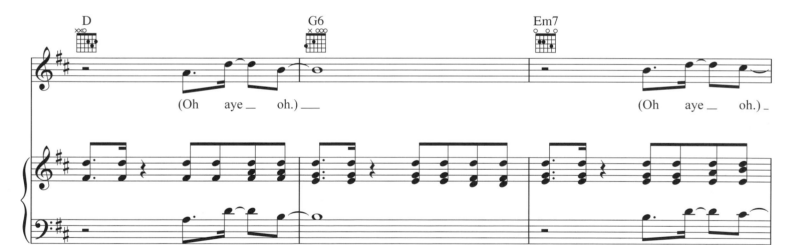

(Oh aye __ oh.) __ (Oh aye __ oh.) __

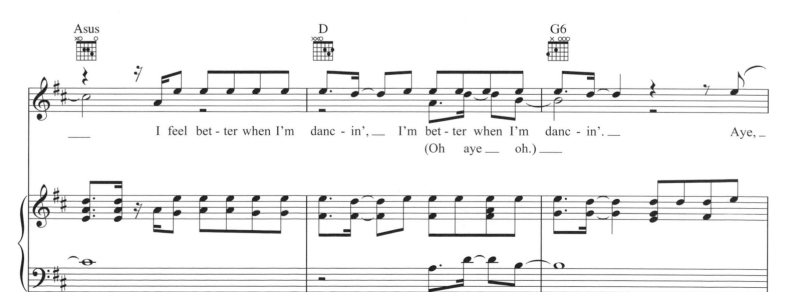

I feel bet - ter when I'm danc - in', __ I'm bet - ter when I'm danc - in'. __ Aye, __
(Oh aye __ oh.) __

GOOD TO BE ALIVE

Words and Music by MEGHAN TRAINOR
and RYAN TRAINOR

I ain't try-in' to think a-bout all my prob-lems; I'm liv-ing now, ___ I'm liv-ing now. ___ I can't sit and wor-ry a-bout the fu-

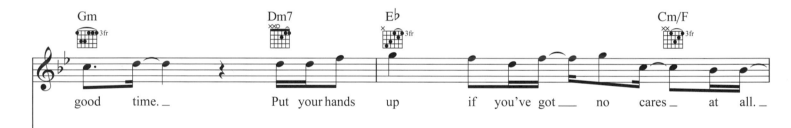

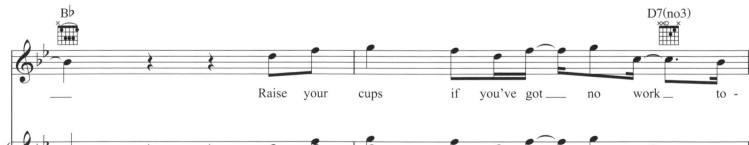

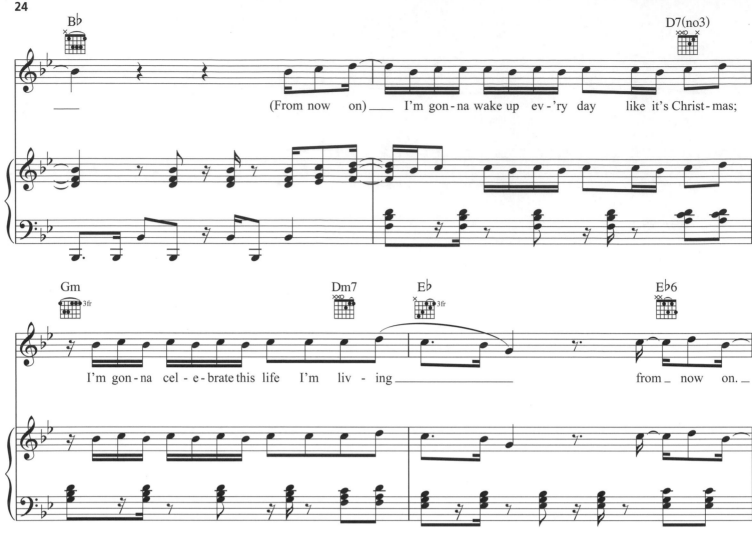

(From now on) ___ I'm gon-na wake up ev-'ry day like it's Christ-mas;

I'm gon-na cel-e-brate this life I'm liv-ing _____ from _ now on. _

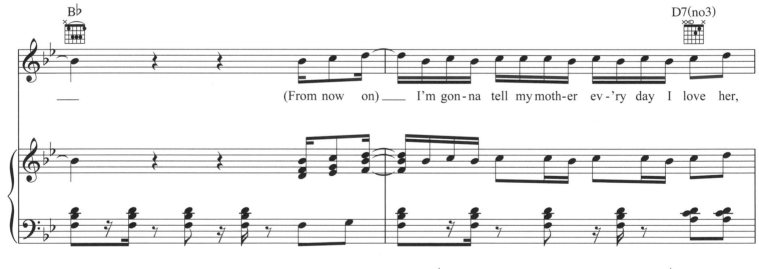

(From now on) ___ I'm gon-na tell my moth-er ev-'ry day I love her,

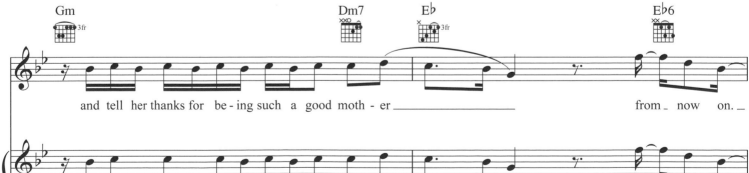

and tell her thanks for be-ing such a good moth-er _____ from _ now on. _

26

You on-ly got one life; live in the mo-ment. It feels good, don't it? It feels good, don't it?

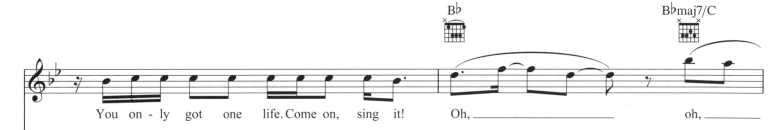

You on-ly got one life; live in the mo-ment. It feels good, don't it? It feels good, don't it?

You on-ly got one life. Come on, sing it! Oh, _____ oh, _____

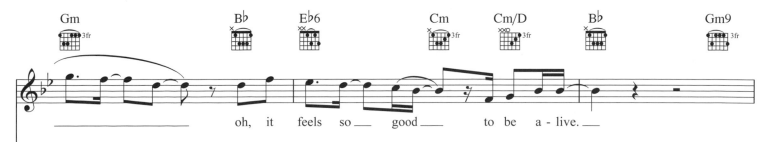

_____ oh, it feels so __ good __ to be a-live. __

Oh, _____ oh, _____ oh, it

feels so ___ good ___ to be a - live. ___ (Come on, sing it!)

It feels good, don't it? It feels good, don't it? You on - ly got one life; live in the mo - ment.

Oh, _____ oh, _____ oh, it

It feels good, don't it? It feels good, don't it? You on-ly got one life; live in the mo-ment.

feels so _ good _ to be a - live. _

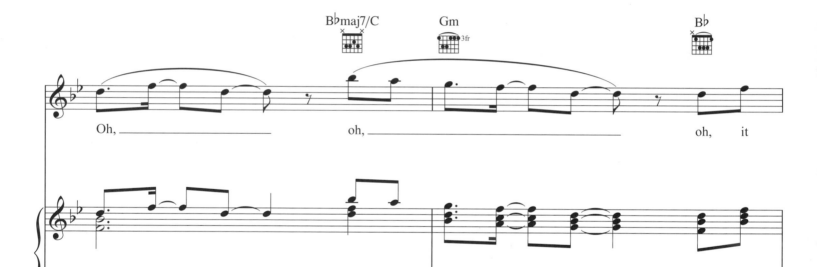

Oh, _ oh, _ oh, it

feels so _ good _ to be a - live. _

THAT'S WHAT I LIKE

Words and Music by TRAMAR DILLARD,
TEEMU BRUNILA, THOMAS TROELSEN,
JIMMY MARINOS, MIKE SKILL,
WALTER PALAMARCHUK, JAMIE SANDERSON,
BREYEN ISAAC, MILES BEARD,
FREDERICK HIBBERT and VINCENT VENDITTO

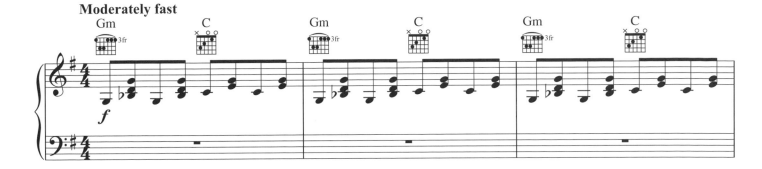

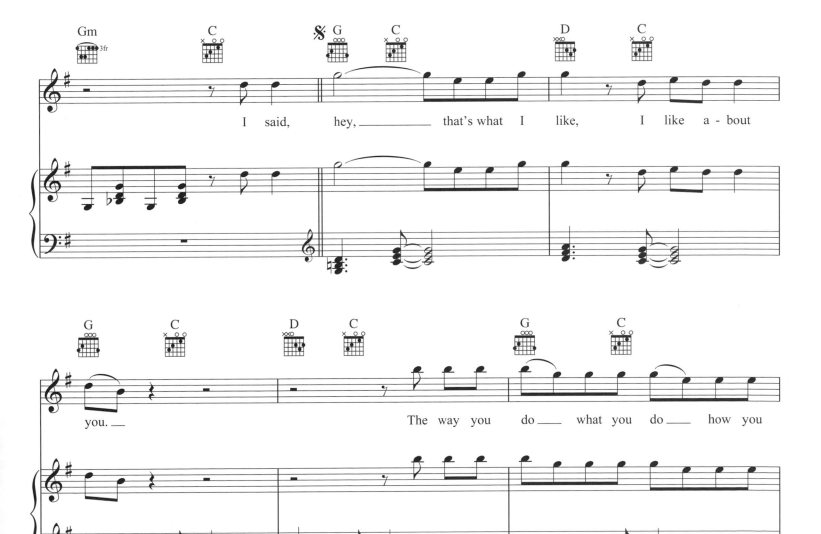

I said, hey, _____ that's what I like, I like a-bout you. ___

The way you do ___ what you do ___ how you

do, _____ I like a-bout you. Come on now,

hey, _____ that's what I like, I like a-bout you. __

The way you do __ what you do __ how you do, __ I like a-bout

you. I said hey, hey, hey, hey.

(Oh, __ Lo-, __ Lord.) __ They call me A - li Boom - ba - yeh.

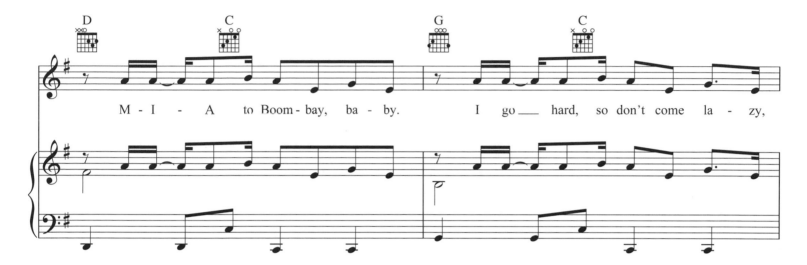

M - I - A to Boom-bay, ba - by. I go __ hard, so don't come la - zy,

come la - zy. This is my par - ty: don't be late.

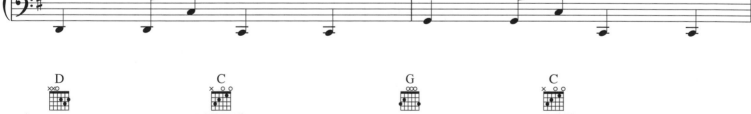

And how much __ fun can one man take? You walk __ past and I go cra - zy.

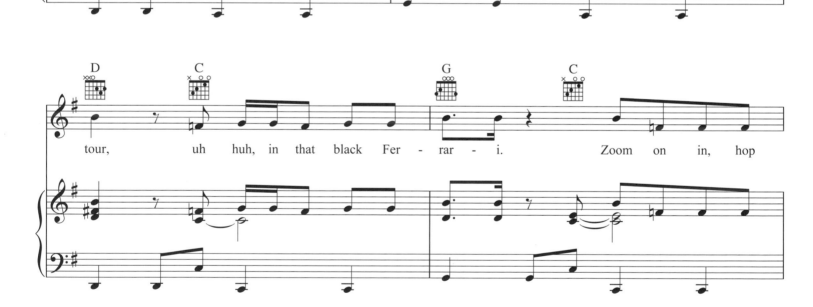

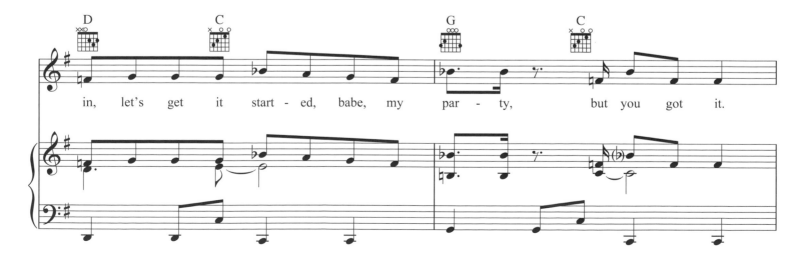

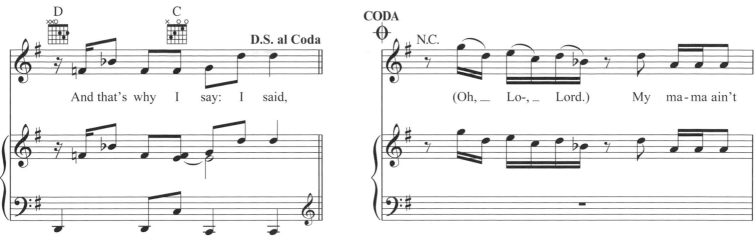

D.S. al Coda

And that's why I say: I said,

CODA

(Oh, ___ Lo-, ___ Lord.) My ma-ma ain't

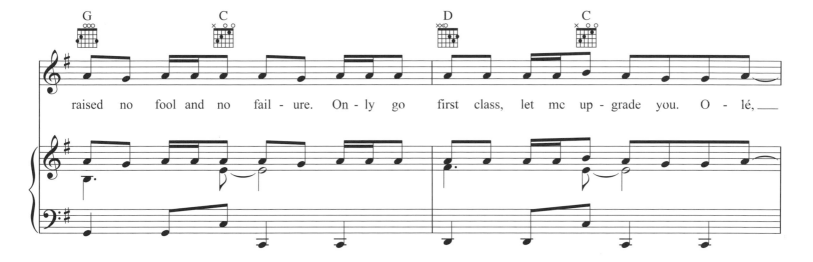

raised no fool and no fail-ure. On-ly go first class, let me up-grade you. O - lé, ___

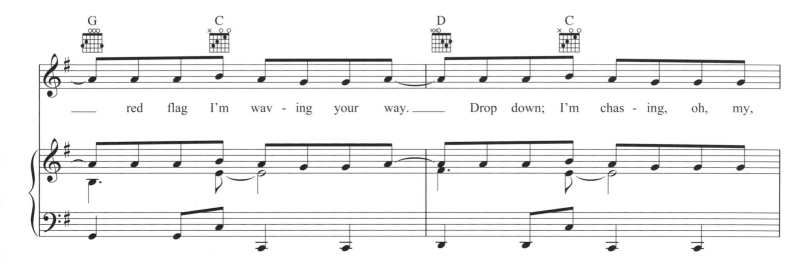

___ red flag I'm wav-ing your way. ___ Drop down; I'm chas-ing, oh, my,

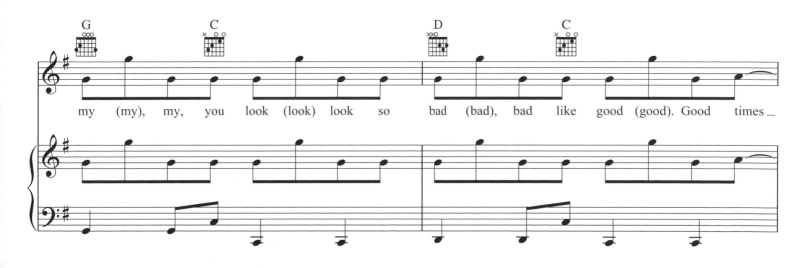

my (my), my, you look (look) look so bad (bad), bad like good (good). Good times ___

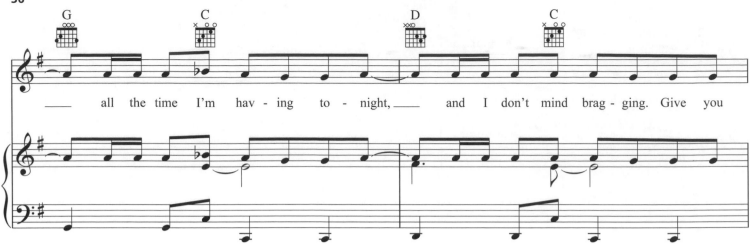

all the time I'm hav-ing to-night,___ and I don't mind brag-ging. Give you

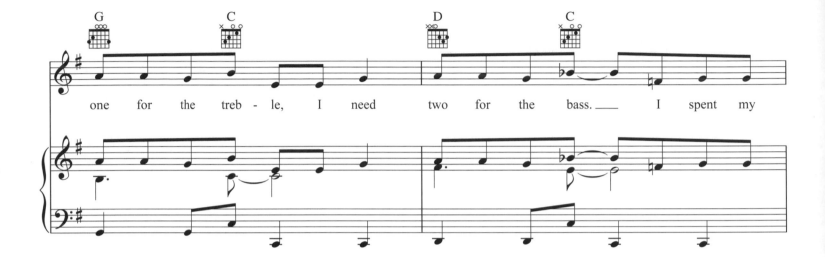

one for the treb-le, I need two for the bass.___ I spent my

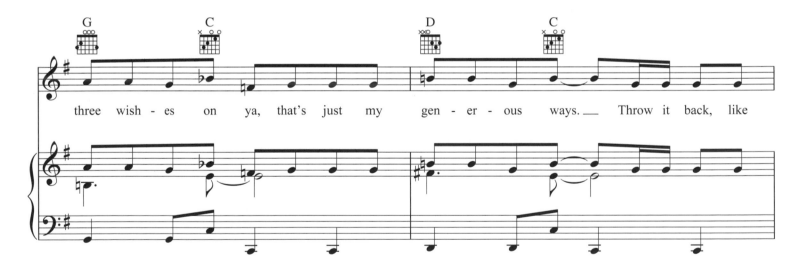

three wish-es on ya, that's just my gen-er-ous ways.___ Throw it back, like

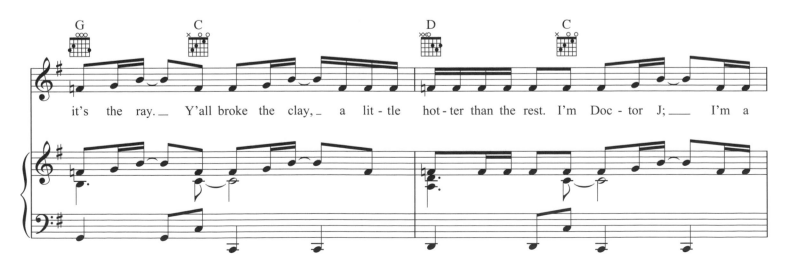

it's the ray.___ Y'all broke the clay,___ a lit-tle hot-ter than the rest. I'm Doc-tor J;___ I'm a

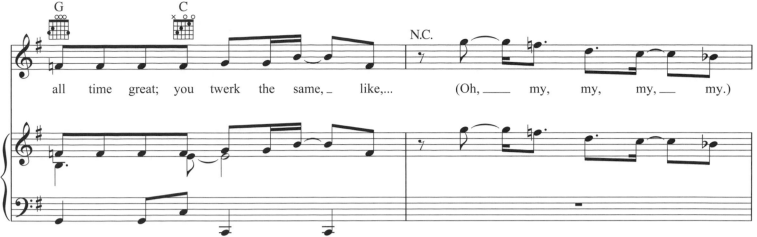

all time great; you twerk the same, _ like,... (Oh, ____ my, my, my, ___ my.)

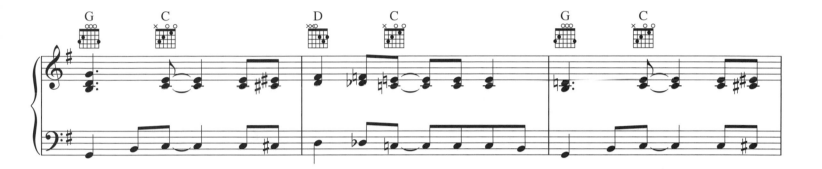

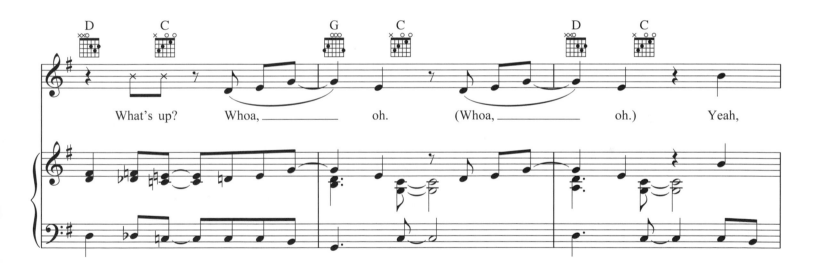

What's up? Whoa, _____ oh. (Whoa, _____ oh.) Yeah,

yeah, yeah, yeah. _ (Yeah, yeah, yeah, yeah.) _ Whoa, _____ whoa, oh. (Whoa, _____

do, ___ I like a-bout you.
(Yeah, ___ that's what I like a-bout you.) Come on now,

do, ___ I like a-bout you.
(Yeah, ___ that's what I like a-bout you.) I said

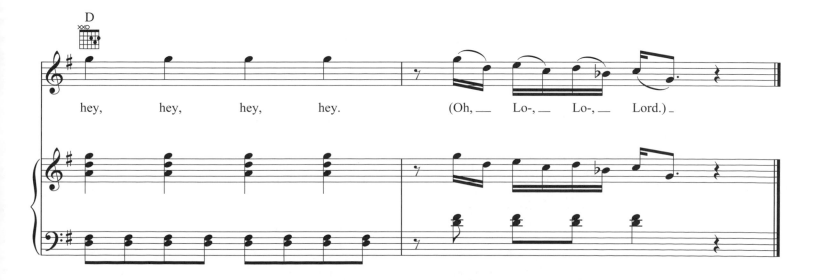

hey, hey, hey, hey. (Oh, ___ Lo-, ___ Lo-, ___ Lord.) ___

SKATING

By VINCE GUARALDI

Bright Jazz Waltz

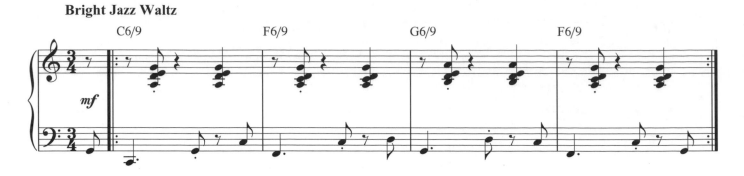

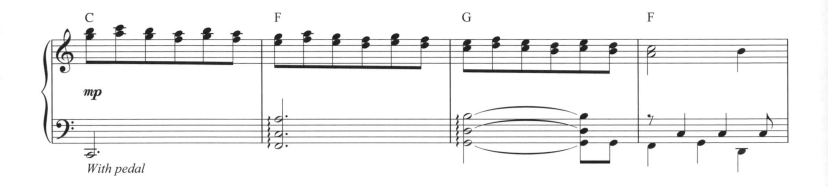

With pedal

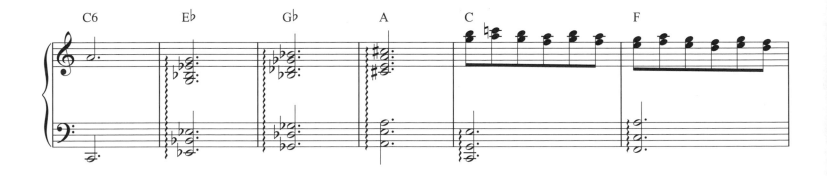

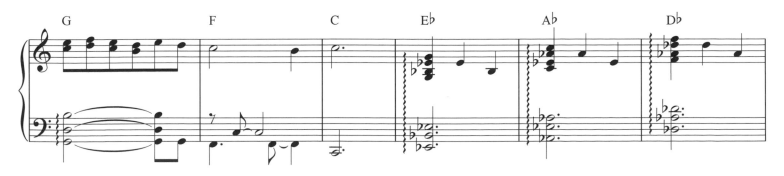

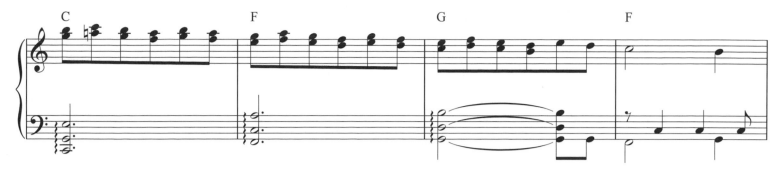

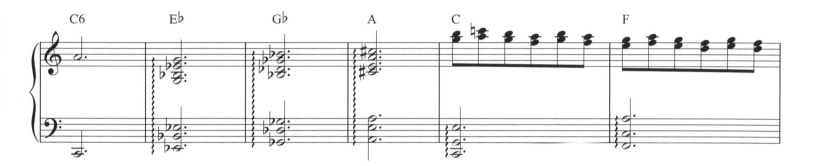

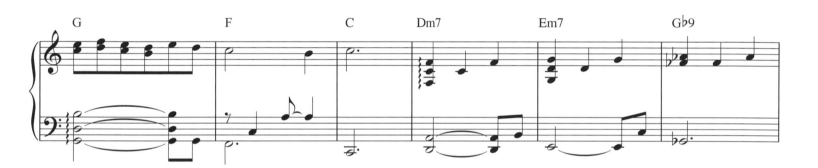

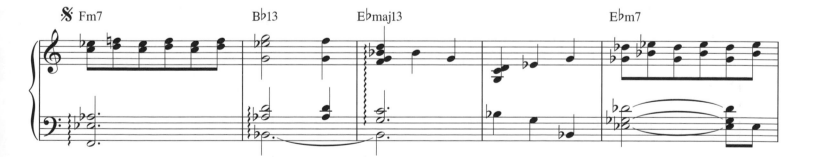

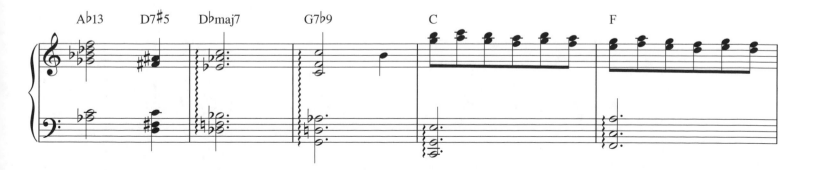

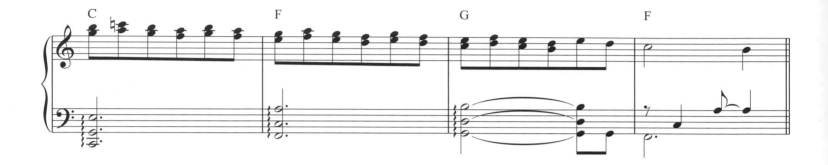

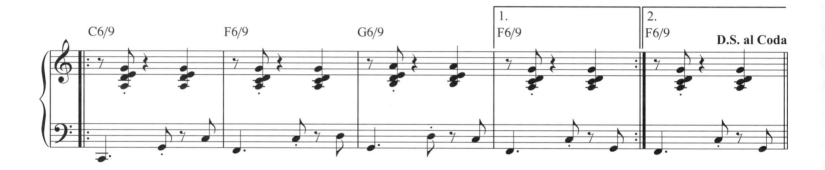

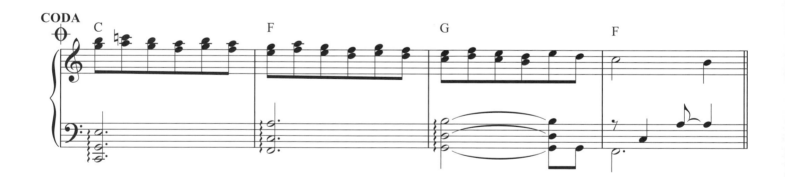

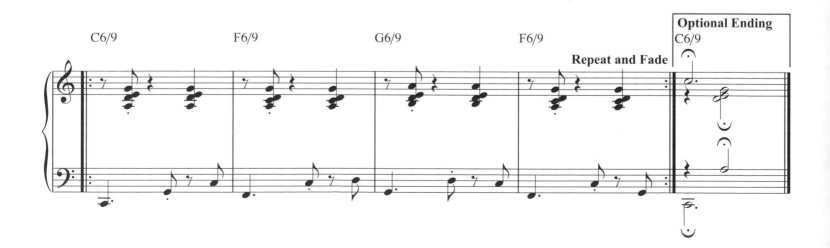

CHRISTMAS TIME IS HERE

Words by LEE MENDELSON
Music by VINCE GUARALDI

Christ-mas time is here, hap-pi-ness and cheer. Fun for all that chil-dren call their fa-v'rite time of year.

Snow-flakes in the air, car-ols ev-'ry-where. Old-en times and an-cient rhymes of love and dreams to share.

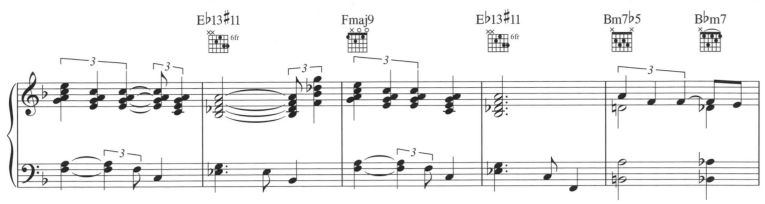

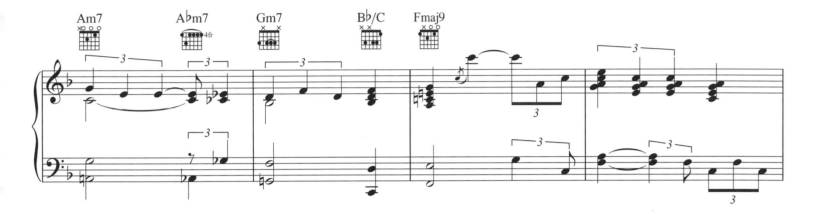

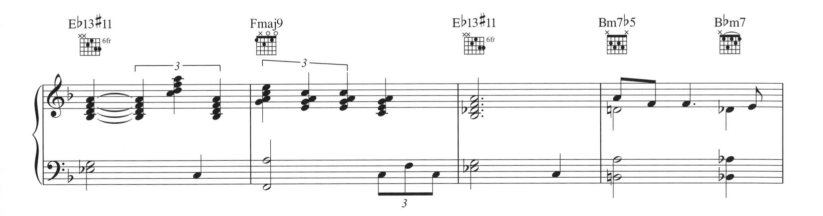

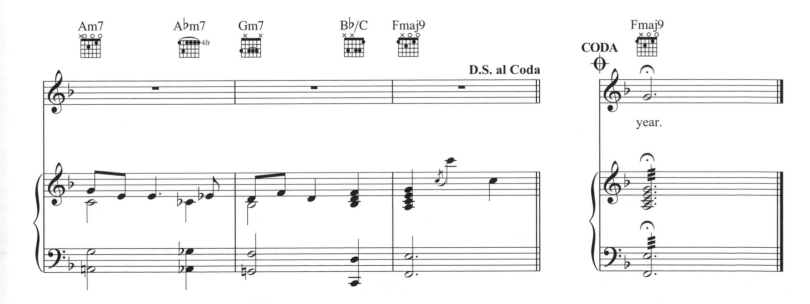

year.

CHARLIE BROWN IN LOVE

Written by CHRISTOPHE BECK
and LEO BIRENBERG

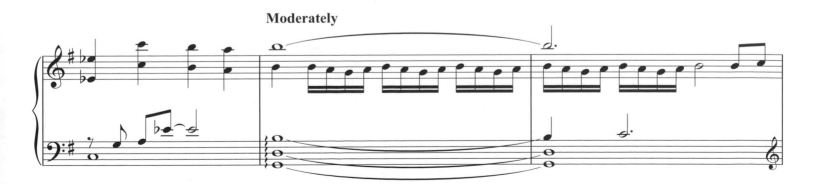

Moderately slow

Moderately

THE LIBRARY

Written by CHRISTOPHE BECK

Quickly

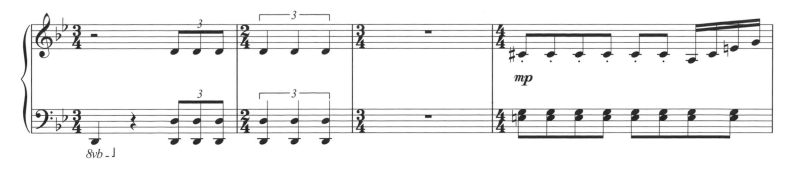

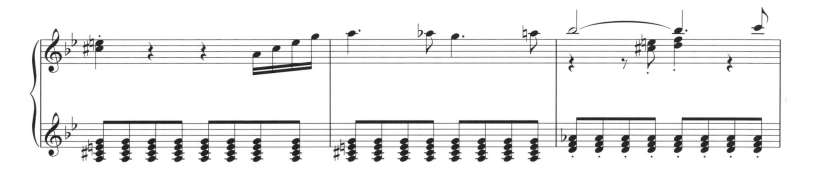

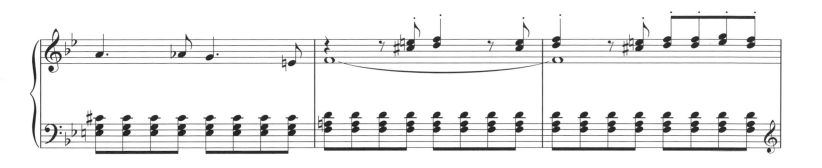

LINUS AND LUCY
(Arranged by Christophe Beck)

By VINCE GUARALDI

Slowly, expressively

p

Pedal ad lib. throughout

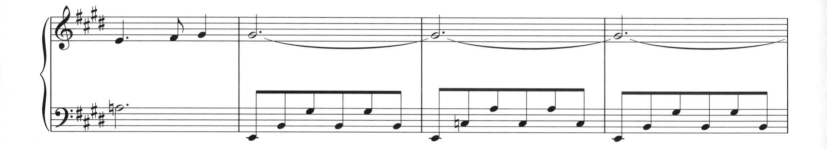